By Bob Garvey & Kim Langridge

Cartoons:
Phil Hailstone

Published by:

Teachers' Pocketbooks
Laurel House, Station Approach,
Alresford, Hampshire SO24 9JH, UK
Tel: +44 (0)1962 735573
Fax: +44 (0)1962 733637
E-mail: sales@teacherspocketbooks.co.uk
Website: www.teacherspocketbooks.co.uk

*Teachers' Pocketbooks is an imprint of
Management Pocketbooks Ltd.*

Series Consultant: **Brin Best**.

As the Mentoring in Schools Pocketbook, first
published in 2003.

This revised re-titled edition,
published in 2006.

British Library Cataloguing-in-Publication Data
– A catalogue record for this book is available
from the British Library.

ISBN-13   978 1 903776 74 2
ISBN-10   1 903776 74 0

Design, typesetting and graphics by Efex Ltd.
Printed in UK

Contents

Overview

The *Pupil Mentoring Pocketbook* replaces the original *Mentoring in Schools Pocketbook*. It deals with:

- Mentoring in general
- Peer mentoring
- Learning mentors
- Voluntary mentoring
- E-mentoring

Some of this book is based on The *Mentoring Pocketbook* from the Management Pocketbooks Series, which is primarily aimed at business mentoring. Teachers who mentor teachers will find The *Mentoring Pocketbook* helpful. Copies of both books would make a useful addition to a school's resources.

How to use this Pocketbook

This book is a resource and support for those involved in mentoring in schools.
It is aimed primarily at teachers (who may also have a mentoring scheme
co-ordinator's role). It will also be useful reading for headteachers, learning mentors,
volunteer mentors, peer mentors, parents and governors.
It can be used in a number of ways:

- **As an outline resource book** with ideas on how to:
  - Set up and manage schemes in a school
  - Train peer mentors
  - Conduct mentoring meetings
  - Evaluate mentoring
  - Persuade people of its benefits
  - Ask relevant questions
  - Avoid problems and pitfalls

How to use this Pocketbook

- **For reflection** – it is a resource to consult when you want to reflect on what has gone on in a session or in the scheme
- **To stimulate the development of mentoring** – the book provides a challenge and stimulus to reflect on mentoring in schools and mentoring schemes
- **For discussion** – the book can be a focus for discussion with people interested in mentoring in schools, eg teachers, pupils, parents and governors
- **To read selectively** – the book is designed to be read in any way you feel appropriate, either from cover to cover or by the sections relevant to you

Note Where this booklet talks of the *mentee* others sometimes use the words *protégé, mentoree, buddy* or *learner*. *Mentee* is our preferred term.

Introduction

The first mentor

Mentoring has a long and illustrious history in education. It is a very human and natural activity that has been around since the Ancient Greeks. The first mentor was the Goddess Athene who worked with Telemachus the son of King Odysseus. Athene took the form of Mentor, the trusted friend and advisor to Odysseus. This is probably the first account of a teacher-pupil relationship. Mentor helped Telemachus to learn how to become a king.

In 17th Century France, the Bishop of Cambrai, Fenelon, wrote 'The Adventures of Telemachus' which is essentially a treatise on educational techniques. The great educational philosopher Rousseau was familiar with Fenelon's work and Rousseau's recommendation on the ideal teacher: pupil ratio was one to one!

Famous mentoring relationships

There are many examples in history of famous mentoring relationships. For example:

- Moses and Joshua
- Lord Cecil and Queen Elizabeth I
- Annie Sullivan and Helen Keller

And recently:

- Alex Ferguson and Wayne Rooney
- Brian Close and Ian Botham
- Peter Thompson and Tony Blair

What is mentoring?

The word 'men' in mentor means 'of the mind'. Defining mentoring, however, is difficult because it takes many different forms and has many different purposes. In recent years it has grown in popularity as a learning and developmental process. Examples of mentoring practice can be found in a whole range of different settings, including schools and business and both the public and the private sectors.

In schools, mentoring can take many different forms and have many different uses ranging from professional development and support for teachers to pupils mentoring pupils. This book is about mentoring pupils in schools. It is based on both research and practical experience.

As authors of this book we are *for* mentoring and recognise that it is a good thing. We have both benefited from mentoring as pupils and as adults. I am sure we can all remember an influential teacher who took an interest in our welfare, learning and development. Bob still remembers John Springall who helped him to return to learning at the age of 14 after he had more or less opted out of school!

What is mentoring?

Mentoring is a learning and developmental relationship between two people.

It involves:

- Personal qualities of commitment, support, challenge
- Drawing on relevant knowledge and experience
- The use of certain skills such as questioning and listening
- Following a process

In mentoring, the relationship between mentor and mentee is all-important.

- The pair develop a high degree of trust and mutual regard
- The mentor helps the pupil become what he or she aspires to be
- The mentor helps the mentee to realise his or her potential

What mentoring pupils isn't

As people who work with mentoring in a range of settings we are concerned that the term 'mentoring' is used to cover many things. For example, 'Academic Mentoring' is a term used in education as a vehicle for improved academic attainment. We are worried by this development because we believe that it is not mentoring but a kind of coaching. In academic coaching, the agenda is with the coach, the school, the local authority, the government – in fact anyone but the pupil!

Mentoring is about working with the learner's agenda and not about the imposition of external agendas and targets. While we agree that raising academic attainment is a good idea, we believe that this is a consequence of good mentoring and not the driver of it.

As adults we often assume that we are acting in the pupil's best interest because 'we know best'. However, it is our experience that if we can really *listen* to the pupil and work with their agenda in the mentoring way, they often achieve far more and beyond our highest expectations. As educators, we are regularly amazed at the willing achievements of the young people we work with.

Mentoring or coaching?

Broadly speaking, the differences between mentoring and coaching can be summed up as:

Mentoring	Coaching
Beyond task or target	Task or target focused
Focus on capability and potential	Focus on skill and performance
Best done by a 'neutral' person or peer	Best done by a teacher, other adult or neutral person
Agenda with learner	Agenda set with or by coach
Reflection encouraged by the learner	Reflections to the learner
Longer term	Shorter term
Feedback intuitive, implicit	Feedback explicit

(adapted from Megginson, D and Clutterbuck, D (2005) *Techniques for Coaching and Mentoring*, Elsevier Butterworth-Heinemann, Oxford)

Uses

Pupil mentoring is employed for a whole variety of reasons, eg to:

- Improve behaviour
- Improve non-attendance
- Unlock hidden talent and potential
- Support study initiatives
- Improve attainment
- Tackle bullying
- For personal and social education
- Build confidence
- Improve the educational environment and experience
- Assist in transition from primary to secondary school
- Engage the educationally disaffected

Scope

Schools are increasingly turning to mentoring to assist and enhance education:

- Pupils are mentoring pupils to the benefit of both parties and the school
- The government is sponsoring *learning mentors* in many inner city schools. How long will it be before this idea is rolled out across all schools?
- Volunteers from business and the community are coming into schools to work with pupils, with great success
- E-mentoring is becoming a central feature in education. The NHS, for example, runs e-mentoring as part of the 'Open Road' Project. This is aimed at supporting pupils in NHS work placements

And, although this is not within the scope of this book, teachers and headteachers are mentoring each other to ease the transition to a new post and assist with continuous professional development.

A mentor's personal qualities

So what makes a good mentor? Someone who is:

- **Enthusiastic** – genuinely interested in the mentee and his/her concerns, needs, dreams and aspirations
- **Motivating and encouraging** – able to channel the mentee's energy into constructive change, new challenges and overcoming difficulties
- **Open** – prepared to share his or her experience of similar issues, be honest about her/himself and honest with the mentee
- **Empathic** – able to appreciate how the mentee thinks, feels and behaves
- **Positive in outlook** – able to appreciate the mentee's point of view and see solutions
- **A good listener** – able to really focus on what the mentee is saying without her personal or his own thoughts crowding out the mentee's words

A mentor's knowledge and experience

A mentor draws on his or her personal experience of:

- Facing difficulties
- Meeting new challenges
- Being helped, being a mentee
- Working with others and contributing
- Achievement, success and failure
- Being responsible for their actions and reactions to others and situations
- Trauma and setback

A mentor's abilities and skills

A mentor is skilled at:

- Assessing the significance of the mentee's story
- Building rapport and trust
- Telling relevant stories
- Listening
- Challenging
- Supporting
- Questioning
- Relating
- Showing empathy

The Mentoring Process

Getting started

The mentoring discussion often follows a process.

Different mentors have different strengths and work in different ways.

A useful framework is a **3-stage model** of helping:

Stage 1 - **Exploration**   Stage 2 - **New understanding**   Stage 3 - **Action planning**

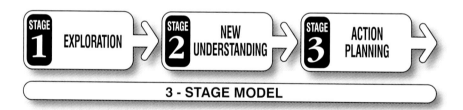

3-stage model

The model can be used in a number of ways:

- To **reflect** upon what mentoring involves
- As a **schedule** for a mentoring meeting – to work through the stages
- As a **map** of the mentoring process – to see what ground has been covered and what needs further attention
- To **reflect** on the mentoring **relationship** over time as the mentee moves towards achieving the goals identified earlier in the mentoring relationship
- To enhance **shared understanding** of the mentoring process and relationship, and to develop the mentee's ability to use the model independently

Stage 1 – Exploration

Strategies a mentor uses:

- Takes the lead
- Clarifies the aims and objectives of the mentoring
- Pays attention to the relationship and develops it
- Supports and counsels

Methods a mentor may use:

- Asks open questions
- Listens
- Negotiates an agenda

How to make the most of Stage 1

The mentor in Stage 1:

- Takes the lead to create rapport
- Establishes ground rules and the relationship's boundaries
- Builds a positive atmosphere that encourages exploration
- Shows commitment to the mentee, the mentoring process and the mentoring relationship
- Gives it time, and is patient
- Helps the mentee to arrive at his or her own answers
- Resists the temptation to give advice or tell the mentee what to do

There are occasions when advice and direction are helpful, but not in Stage 1. Action plans come unstuck when rushed and insufficient exploration leads to faulty understanding in Stage 2.

What a mentor might say/ask in Stage 1

How long does Stage 1 last?

This is an important question. But, it does not have a straightforward answer.
It is important to have some idea of how much time to give to exploring an issue so that the mentor can assess progress.

Much depends on the topic being explored.

If it is something significant, related to changes in personal attitudes and behaviours, the pair may explore an issue on and off for about two to three months.

If it is a practical topic related to knowledge or skills it may take a few minutes or a few hours.

If a mentor or mentee feels stuck in a rut of endless exploration with no progress, it is time to talk about the relationship!

Stage 2 – new understanding

Strategies a mentor uses:

- Supports and questions
- Gives constructive feedback
- Coaches and demonstrates skills

Methods a mentor may use:

- Listens and challenges
- Asks open and closed questions
- Recognises strengths and weaknesses
- Establishes priorities
- Identifies learning needs
- Gives information and advice
- Shares experiences and tells stories

How to make the most of Stage 2

A mentor in Stage 2 is:

- Flexible and resourceful
- Ready to move forward (and sometimes backwards) empathically and constructively with the mentee
- Offers encouragement
- Doesn't rush and is patient
- Ready to return to Stage 1 if necessary
- Supportive, sensitive and challenging
- Able to share a relevant story

Stage 2 is the **turning point** in the process. New understanding often releases energy and can be exciting but it can also be uncomfortable. The mentee may be resistant in which case progress can be slow and erratic. This could signal the need for more exploration. New learning can make the mentee feel vulnerable, especially if it requires recognition that old ways of behaving are not helpful to them and there is a need to change.

What a mentor might say/ask in Stage 2

'What is there to learn here, what's the most important thing to work on, now that you're seeing the situation differently?'

'You've done really well but there are also things you've done that you regret. Is that a fair comment?'

'Now that doing X looks like a good option, I could tell you what I did once in a similar situation.'

'Well done, that feels like a breakthrough.'

'So, if someone did that to you, how would you feel?'

'The way you're talking now reminds me of the time I.....'

How long does Stage 2 last?

Reaching new understandings is key to a successful final stage. Action from poor understanding is always flawed! This stage should not be rushed, but reaching a new understanding can happen quite spontaneously, even during a Stage 1 discussion.

Equally it may take hours, days, weeks, months and possibly years to fully understand a complex issue.

The timescale is dependent on experience, the nature and complexity of the issue and the quality of the conversations in the mentoring discussions.

Stage 3 – action planning

Strategies a mentor uses:

- Examines options for action and their consequences
- Attends to the mentoring process and the relationship
- Negotiates an action plan

Methods a mentor uses:

- Encourages new and creative ways of thinking
- Helps to make decisions and solves problems
- Agrees action plans
- Monitors progress and evaluates outcomes

How to make the most of Stage 3

In Stage 3 a mentor:

- Gives advice and direction sparingly
- Gains commitment to change
- Agrees targets
- Looks after the relationship
- Affirms and celebrates progress

When Stages 1 and 2 are done thoroughly, Stage 3 is usually straightforward and, often, the mentee can see what to do for themselves.

Plans are followed through when the mentee owns the solution.

Not every meeting ends in an action plan. Sometimes the action will be to meet again, and that will be progress enough.

What a mentor might say/ask in Stage 3

How long does Stage 3 last?

It can be very tempting to rush to action. This is often true when there is a lot of pressure on the mentee to change their behaviour.

The quality of action is firmly linked to the quality of Stages 1 and 2.

Sometimes the action phase is immediate, but with complex attitudinal and behavioural issues it may take weeks, months or even years to fully develop.

Mentoring can be about *quick fixes* but if it is to really work well a longer-term view is necessary.

STAGE 1 EXPLORATION → STAGE 2 NEW UNDERSTANDING → STAGE 3 ACTION PLANNING →

3 - STAGE MODEL

Training and support – for the mentor

Whatever scheme you are running, it is important that both mentors and mentees have some training and support. These aspects are referred to in specific sections of the book but here are a few general pointers.

The **mentor** needs to know and understand:

- What is expected
- How to ask open questions
- About the 3-stage model
- The importance of listening
- The importance of ground rules and boundaries
- The difference between confidentiality and secrecy

The mentor needs to have an opportunity to practise these skills and abilities in a risk-free environment.

The mentor will need ongoing support.

Training and support – for the mentee

The **mentee** will need to know and understand:

- What is expected
- The importance of ground rules
- The difference between confidentiality and secrecy
- About the 3-stage model
- The importance of being open to feedback

Evaluation

Why evaluate?

Periodic reviews are often invaluable in providing feedback and hard data about how things are working, as well as justifying the continued allocation of resources for the scheme.

Whatever type of scheme you are running, there is always a need to evaluate. The following section provides guidance on how to go about it regardless of the type of scheme.

Evaluation

Evaluation need not be time-consuming or complicated; it is, after all, simply a means to measure three component parts of the scheme:

1. **Input**   This will take the form of training and ongoing support
2. **Output**   This is the activity that results from the above input
3. **Impact**   What has changed?

Ask these questions to help decide how to go about evaluating the scheme:

- What are we measuring?
- How can we measure it in the quickest and simplest way?
- What are we going to do with the results?

What are we measuring?

Evaluation can employ one or both of the accepted approaches to information gathering.

A **quantitative** approach involves gathering hard facts and data. In the context of mentoring, this can take the form of asking closed questions such as:
- *'How many times did you meet?'*
- *'Did you set clear learning goals?'*
- *'Was an action plan developed?'*

In contrast, a **qualitative** approach involves asking more open-ended questions to find out what the person thinks or feels about the experience.
These can take form of:
- *'Has mentoring made a difference to you?'*
- *'What are these differences?'*
- *'What have you liked about the scheme?'*
- *'What haven't you liked?'*

Often, when we evaluate something we use a mix of styles to enable us to build a picture of what has happened and how effective it has been in meeting the aims and objectives of the mentoring activity.

Measuring success through questioning

You will need to gather information at specific points in time. Gather the information from mentors, mentees, parents, teachers and, in voluntary schemes, the employers.

Mentor training and mentee briefing

'Was the venue ok?' 'Did everyone have a clear idea about what mentoring is and what was expected of them?' 'How could the training/briefing be improved?'

After the relationship has started

'How often do they meet?' 'Have goals been agreed and is everyone comfortable with them?' 'Have they established ground rules and boundaries?' 'Are there any issues of concern?'

Measuring success through questioning (cont'd)

Mid-term/relationship

'Are things changing because of the mentoring?' 'What is working well?' 'What support is still needed?' 'Are there any problems?' 'How can these be addressed?'

Close

'What difference has mentoring made?' 'What has changed?' 'How do both parties feel about it?' 'Did they match their goals?' 'How did the goals change and evolve?' 'What can be done now that couldn't be done at the beginning?'

What are we going to do with the results?

Keep the evaluation clear, brief and user-friendly. It can be circulated to interested parties such as the governors, teaching staff, pupils, parents, Local Education Authority and, even, the local press. This will:

- Assist in raising the profile of mentoring
- Help to acknowledge people's contributions
- Thank those involved
- Bring credit to the school and its pupils

Codes of practice

All mentoring schemes should have a code of practice. This is often best created by those involved so that it takes into account the specific circumstances of the mentoring arrangements.

In general, a code of practice should specify how everybody involved in the mentoring can expect to be treated and how they should treat others.

More specifically, voluntary and learning mentor schemes will need to cover issues relating to child protection and the law. Guidance on procedural best practice, with reference to both the mentor's and the mentee's rights (right of privacy etc), should also be included.

Boundaries and ethical issues

The role of the mentor has often been described as being a *professional friend*. This is especially so when mentoring a young pupil.

Having agreed boundaries in the relationship stops the mentoring becoming intrusive for both the mentor and mentee alike. For example, there should be no obligation to disclose anything that is not relevant to the mentoring discussion and **no** reason why either party should have the other's home details or phone number.

Confidentiality

Any mentoring session has to be confidential but confidentiality always has a boundary to it. If there is no boundary, the content of the relationship may become based on secrecy or conspiracy. This is not appropriate behaviour in mentoring. If the mentee steps over the boundary, then this needs to be discussed and a third party may become involved. In most cases this requires a degree of judgement on behalf of the mentor, eg:

- If the mentee is bullying another pupil, it may be appropriate for the mentor to maintain confidentiality for a while to help the mentee come to a new understanding of the situation. In this way the mentee may learn to change his or her behaviour with the support of the mentor.

- In another, more extreme, situation, the mentee may disclose that they are doing something illegal or that they have been subject to some form of abuse from a relative. In these situations, confidentiality within the mentoring pair cannot be maintained and a referral to a third party is essential. However, it is vital to try and gain agreement from the mentee for this referral first.

Introduction

 The Mentoring Process

 Peer Mentors ◀

 Volunteer Mentors

 Learning Mentors

 E-Mentoring

 Further Information

Peer Mentors

What is peer mentoring?

'It's about students supporting students.'
Headteacher

'Peer mentoring is when you work with someone in your own year group or below and build a relationship of trust and respect.'
Year 10 mentor

'It helps young people understand the demands and expectations put on them when they start a new school, through to taking public examinations and everything in between.'
Peer mentoring co-ordinator

Views from pupils and teachers

'I was really scared when I came to the big school but my mentor was really friendly and helped me find my way around.'
Year 7 mentee

'Even if I'm down they come over and ask me how I'm doing.'
Year 8 mentee

'I didn't like it when I came up to the big school so now I want to try and make it better for the younger kids.'
Year 10 mentor

'Teachers don't always understand what the kids are on about - we are closer to their age.'
Year 11 mentor

'Mentors give an insider's guide to school life.'
Teacher

'Youngsters now have a stake in their own school.'
Form teacher

What can it be called?

Peer mentoring can be known as:

- Buddying
- Peer tutoring
- Peer educating
- One-to-one tutoring

How does peer mentoring work?

There are many variations including:

- Pupils in both primary and secondary schools can volunteer to be a mentor or mentee following an assembly on the topic
- Some schools allocate mentors to a class and allow potential mentees to choose their own mentor. Others will allocate a mentor with particular subject skills or because they are a positive role model
- In some schools all newcomers have access to either a class mentor or an individual mentor should they want one
- Other schools favour schemes for gifted pupils. Some provide an extra layer of support for those who are falling behind or experiencing problems with school in general
- Secondary schools often draw on students in year 9 or above for their mentors
- Primary schools may draw on year 6 pupils for their mentors

All mentors are trained and supported by the scheme co-ordinator, year tutor or form tutor who acts as a mentor and guide to the peer mentors.

How does it work from the pupils' perspective?

- They speak the same language as each other
- Have common experiences
- Mentors have high levels of empathy with the mentees
- They share common issues, hopes and fears

Credibility and facts, empathy and support

Issues such as sex, relationships, drugs and alcohol are often discussed in young people's groups based on gossip, myth and hearsay. But, a trained peer mentor can provide factual information on these topics effectively and with more credibility than adults.

Schools often have clear anti-bullying strategies but children being bullied can feel very isolated and lonely. Peer mentors can offer the bridge between school policy and personal experiences.

The transition to *big school* is often on the agenda in peer mentoring relationships.

Linking the school's agenda to the pupils' agenda

Effort must be made to find a link between the school's agenda and the pupils' agenda. For example, the school may be interested in issues such as study skills, homework, behaviour, attendance, bullying and health issues. Pupils may have a different perspective, which could be about relationships with friends, a pet dying, sexual experiences, boredom, not seeing the relevance of schoolwork or problems at home.

If the focus is on the **school's** agenda there is a risk of the mentee being put off.

When the focus is initially on the **mentee's** agenda, this will help to build trust, rapport and confidence. The mentee will start to feel valued and respected. Increased self-esteem, confidence and motivation follow and, ultimately, the school's and the mentee's objectives coincide and are achieved.

Main topics of discussion in peer mentoring

- Bullying – physical, verbal, at school or at home
- Relationships, peer pressure
- Smoking, drinking, sex, drugs
- Changing bodies, general health issues
- Relationship with parents, family break-up, bereavement, redundancy
- Homework, relationships with teachers
- Difficulties with school subjects
- Self-image, food and diet

Setting up a peer mentoring scheme

Why do schemes fail?

- Insufficient resources
- Lack of planning
- No clear aim or objectives
- Lack of staff support
- Lack of support for the mentors
- No training

Voices of experience

'The more time spent thinking about the scheme the better. You need to think about who it is for and what you want it to achieve. You also need to know how you will know when you have achieved it.'
Experienced scheme co-ordinator

'I found it really useful to write an action plan and to think about who else inside or outside the school needed to be informed or involved.'
Scheme co-ordinator

'Some staff couldn't imagine that the pupils could be trained to deal with complex and sensitive issues such as sexual health and substance abuse and they have been surprised at the attitudes, maturity and skill of the young mentors.'
Head of year

'We found our local EBP (Education Business Partnership, see pages 75 & 109) really helpful and supportive.'
Headteacher

'We are trying to develop community spirit and relationships within the school.'
Scheme co-ordinator

7 steps to a successful peer mentoring scheme

1. Clear aim and objectives
2. Promoting and gaining support for mentoring
3. Recruiting mentors and mentees
4. Training mentors and mentees
5. Matching mentors with mentees
6. Supporting the mentors during the relationship
7. Evaluating the relationships and celebrating the successes

The next few pages give more detail on the above points.

Aim and objectives

The aim of the scheme must be linked to the strategic goals of the school (the big picture). It should inform parents/carers, teachers, pupils and governors about the purpose of peer mentoring and what it needs to achieve.

The objectives must be linked to tangible benefits and outcomes, which can be either clearly demonstrated to a third party or measured numerically.

For example:

- Better attendance figures
- Improved self-esteem
- Better time-keeping
- Increased participation in school activities
- Reduced school exclusions
- Increased motivation

Promoting and gaining support

It is very important to promote and gain support for a mentoring scheme.

Ask:

- Who has an interest in the scheme's success?
- What are their interests and motivations?
- How do we use their interest to enlist their support?
- How do we keep their support?
- Who are the potential participants?
- What are their motivations?
- How do we link their motivations to the scheme?
- How do we approach them?
- How do we give feedback on the progress?
- How can we use the participants' language to communicate the mentoring message to the mentees?

Recruitment

It is important to link the recruitment policy to the scheme's aim and objectives.

Ask:

- Who are the potential mentors?
- Is mentoring focusing on specific groups?
- Is mentoring open to all?
- Who are the potential mentees?
- Are they from specific groups?

Note If the scheme is open to all in a class or year group, there is less risk of alienating students or of reinforcing stereotypes (ie: mentoring only happens if you are bright, bad or less able).

Recruiting options

Being a peer mentor often becomes a prestigious role in the school.
Recruit mentors who:

- Have recognised ability in working with others
- Are positive role models
- Have overcome problems
- Can focus on a variety of activities

Take care not to appoint on academic ability alone. Some schools have had very
positive results in recruiting under-achieving pupils from years 9 and 10 as mentors.
They go into feeder schools and work with year 6 pupils on literacy and numeracy.
This often helps to improve the mentors' self-esteem and level of achievement, while
assisting year 6 pupils in their transition by:

- Starting to build relationships in the secondary school
- Having their concerns about the transition addressed
- Building their confidence

Mentoring is reciprocal in its benefits.

Training

Who is going to deliver the training?

The best person to deliver the training is often an outside person or a non-teaching member of staff. This can create a more relaxed and open first-name environment for the mentors. Sometimes past mentors can be involved.

How long will it be?

Sessions can be spread over a period of time, say one period per week for six weeks, or a full-day-off timetable can work equally well.

Training

What is the content of the training?

The mentors will need to:

- Know the purpose of the scheme
- Learn what mentoring is and is not
- Understand and apply the 3-stage model (see pages 20 to 33)
- Know their responsibilities and the boundaries of the mentoring activity
- Know where and who to go to for help
- Understand the difference between confidentiality and secrecy
- Practise listening and questioning skills

Who needs to be involved?

- Parents need to know about the scheme, their child's involvement and the benefits of participating
- The person in the school responsible for the timetable
- The mentees will need a presentation from the mentors following their training

Training

Where is training to be held?

On site is easier but it is important to think about giving a positive message to mentors. A nice room with comfortable chairs is a good start.

What resources will you need?

Resources may include:

- Flipchart, pens and paper
- Video, DVD, TV, computer
  (see Further Information)
- Video camera
- Evaluation sheet. (Keep this simple: What did you enjoy? What didn't you enjoy? How could the training be improved?)

Matching mentors with mentees

Points to consider:

- Gender
- Ethnicity
- Skills and knowledge
- Experience
- The issues

There are no rules here and *same gender* can work as well as *different gender* – it depends on the people, the situation and the issues. Above all, our evidence is that the starting point should be that each mentee has a trained mentor who is willing to commit to listening and working with him/her.

Supporting the mentors

Mentors need:

- Regular review meetings together to discuss common issues and problems

- Support material – books, videos, etc

- Access to the scheme co-ordinator (who needs to make an effort to keep in contact with individual mentors)

- Opportunities for **celebration** to recognise the work and commitment of the peer mentors – a trip out of school, a party or something more formal such as a certificate of achievement

It can also help to meet with mentors in other schools to share practice and ideas. Sometimes mentors may give talks to other schools interested in mentoring.

Other benefits of peer mentoring

- Manages transition to *big* school
- Increases self-esteem and confidence
- Supports study skills
- Develops *key skills* in mentors
- Contributes to spiritual, health, and moral education (PSE)
- Enhances anti-bullying strategies

Introduction

 The Mentoring Process

 Peer Mentors

 Volunteer Mentors ◀

 Learning Mentors

 E-Mentoring

 Further Information

Volunteer Mentors

What is a volunteer mentor?

Volunteer mentoring has become the most common form of pupil mentoring in schools over the past 10 years. The Home Office Active Community Unit and the DfES both define the role of volunteer mentors in schools as:

A one-to-one, non-judgmental relationship in which an individual mentor voluntarily gives time to support and encourage another person. This relationship is typically developed at a time of transition in the mentee's life, and lasts for a significant and sustained period of time.

In schools, *a significant and sustained period of time* is linked to:

- The age of the pupil
- The problems they may be encountering
- The type of support they need

We were all teenagers once. If we think back, we can usually recall the issues and problems we experienced. Volunteer mentors provide impartial support and guidance during this formative period of a young person's life.

What is a volunteer mentor?

In practice, voluntary mentoring may last for a school term, school year or even longer. It has the same key features as the other forms of mentoring mentioned in this book. These are:

- Defined and confidential
- Operates in a climate of mutual respect and trust
- Has to be linked to the issues important to the mentee
- Mentors are not there to teach or enforce school policy but through the good use of questioning and listening skills, they help the youngster to find their own answer or solution

Who volunteers and why?

Mentors volunteer either from the local community or nearby organisations. They may be unemployed, semi-retired, retired, running their own business, working in a large corporate environment or employed by the local authority. Volunteer mentors can come from anywhere!

Their reasons for volunteering may include:

- They had such a good time at school they want to share the experience
- They had such a bad time at school they don't want anyone else to go through what they did
- They want to share their life experiences and skills
- They want to share their passion for a particular subject or sport
- Someone helped them in their early career and they want to do the same
- They wish that someone had been there for them when they were young

In other words, volunteer mentors come from all walks of life but are united by a common desire to make a positive difference to a young person's life.

Who volunteers and why?

This desire to make a positive difference to a young person's life is, however, not enough in itself. Schools have a responsibility to do everything reasonably possible to ensure the safety of the pupils entrusted to their care and this applies to volunteer mentoring just as it does to the proper maintenance of the building.

Schemes must have a screening process – just as if volunteers were job applicants. This should include:
- An application form with full employment record
- An interview
- References from current/past employers or professionals
- A positive *disclosure* report from the Criminal Records Bureau (CRB)

These safeguards can be complemented by a job description provided by the school. This should:
- Outline the mentor's role and responsibilities
- Set guidelines on conduct
- Have a code of practice

The Criminal Records Bureau (CRB)

The CRB enables the school to clearly establish whether or not a volunteer:

- Is who they say they are
- Is on the sex offenders' register
- Has any spent or unspent convictions

Having a spent/unspent conviction does not necessarily rule anyone out from being an effective and professional mentor. Scheme co-ordinators will need to examine the nature of the offence and the time lapsed. This information can then be weighed against their knowledge of the youngster(s) to be mentored and an informed decision can be made about the prospective mentor's suitability.

Recruiting people with a troubled past

There are numerous schemes that actively look to recruit mentors with a troubled past but who are now reformed. These mentors can often speak with real authority about issues such as substance abuse or joy riding in stolen cars. They can often dispel a number of myths about such behaviour and underline the very real consequences of these activities.

In these situations, the *reformed mentors* are strong role models. They demonstrate that everyone has choices and they are proof that changes in behaviour are possible.

Some schools may be reluctant to take on such mentors. In the end, the school is responsible for the welfare of pupils and the scheme co-ordinator must feel confident that they have made every effort to ensure the safety of pupils, whilst creating a real learning environment.

Views on volunteer mentoring

'My mentor showed me that I didn't have to joy ride and helped me to build a new life for myself.'
A young former joy rider

'My mentor really seemed to care, if you know what I mean. And that made me want to be something different.'
A young former drug abuser

'A volunteer mentor is not a substitute teacher or parent, but is there to offer advice and share life's experience with no other agenda than wanting to assist that person to realise their potential!'
Headteacher

'My mentor helped me to see that I didn't have to go down that path because she had been down there herself and it wasn't very good.'
A year 11 mentee

How to get started

Volunteers mentoring in schools can happen through a number of different routes:

- Accessing support through the local office of the Education Business Partnership (EBP) – national office listed in *Further information*

- Partnership with local employer/s who can recruit mentors from their staff and support them to visit the school regularly

- Partnering with a national agency that offers mentoring to achieve specific aims, such as increased health awareness, reduced substance abuse or students taking up engineering/science careers (see page 110)

- Linking up with local community initiatives such as raising achievement levels in targeted minority groups or dealing with social issues such as drugs

It is a good idea to use your existing network of other local schools to find out who else has a scheme running and how they went about setting it up. Time is a valuable resource and there is little virtue in re-inventing the wheel!

Benefits of volunteer mentors

For the school:

- Provides individual support
- Can support pupils at all stages of development
- Assists in developing career plans
- Enables the school to focus on educational issues
- Supports achievement of school goals and targets

For the mentee:

- Having a positive role model
- Builds confidence and self-esteem
- Builds problem-solving skills
- Introduction to the world of work
- Helps develop self-awareness

Views from the mentees

'Thank you for being so kind and listening to me.'
Year 10 pupil

'Every kid should have one.'
Year 11 pupil

'I'm not sure how it helped, but I smile more.'
Year 8 pupil

'She keeps me out of trouble just by talking with me.'
Year 10 pupil at risk of exclusion

Benefits for the mentor

For the mentor:
- Making a contribution to the community
- Develops questioning and listening skills
- Increases awareness of diversity issues
- Enhances personal self-esteem and motivation

For the businesses:
- Raises corporate profile
- Selling point in recruiting new staff
- Improves staff retention
- Builds interpersonal skills in the organisation

Views from volunteer mentors

'I was terrified at first that it might fail but I have really enjoyed it.'

'I'm putting something back into my community; it's making a real difference to me as well as my mentee.'

'We now have people asking at interviews if we are involved in the local community; it says a lot about your values as a business.'

'It took a while for Terry to open up and we still have periods of silence but it's OK. It's his time without any more pressure and he leaves our meetings relaxed and feeling more in charge of his life.'

Setting up a scheme

There may be any number of reasons why schools will set up or join a voluntary scheme. Typically, these may be:

- As part of the school's anti-bullying strategy
- To increase health awareness which might be related to drugs, sex, diet, smoking and/or sport
- To improve attendance, behaviour and motivation
- To prepare youngsters for a career or employment
- To raise achievement levels for targeted groups

Experienced views

'Mentoring is a very robust tool and schools would be well advised to use mentoring in a number of situations and with a broad range of pupils.'
A headteacher

'If supposedly problem kids are the only bit of the mentoring, then mentoring will get known in the school as something that only happens if you are thick or bad.'
A young mentee

'Treat the mentors exactly as you would expect to be treated if you were giving up your time to assist someone else achieve their goals.'
Voluntary mentor scheme co-ordinator

'Time should also be spent in briefing the mentees about mentoring and how the mentor's role differs from that of parents and teachers and, critically, how confidentiality is different from keeping a secret – many pupils see them as being the same.'
Voluntary mentor scheme co-ordinator

Getting the scheme going and keeping it going

There are a number of organisations that can provide assistance in getting started, such as the Mentoring and Befriending foundation and EBP (see pages 109 and 110). They will give guidance and recommend best practice for starting a scheme.

No matter how much support you receive in setting your scheme up, it is critical that the school has ownership of the mentoring scheme and appoints their own in-house co-ordinator.

The biggest cause of volunteer mentoring relationships breaking down is lack of communication between the school and the volunteer mentor. The co-ordinator needs to be able to:

- Liaise with form tutors or heads of year about time off the timetable
- Contact the volunteer mentor if the pupil is not in school or available for a meeting

Getting the scheme going and keeping it going

Nothing is more dispiriting for a mentor than, having taken time out of their busy day, to arrive at the school to discover that the mentee is not there. There have even been cases of the mentor phoning the day of the meeting to confirm it, only to discover that the mentee has not been in school all week!

So, maintain good communications between:

- The mentee and form tutor/year head about meetings
- The school and the mentor (and, of course, the mentor and school, should the mentor have a problem attending a meeting)
- The scheme co-ordinator and contact person in the organisation or community group

Training the mentors

In addition to the normal key elements of a mentor training programme, mentors and schools will find it beneficial to spend time looking at the following:

- Related child protection issues
- Limits of mentors' responsibilities
- Introduction to the school and school life today – this should include a tour of the school and guidance on current terminologies used in schools
- Likely issues and relevant contacts in the school and community

Supporting the mentors

Mentor development doesn't end with the training but should be ongoing. Mentors are often both enthusiastic and slightly apprehensive when completing their training. Enthusiastic because they want to make a difference to a young person's life and apprehensive because of the possible barriers they may encounter working with someone of a different generation and/or culture. Questions such as, *What if they don't like me and don't talk?* or *What if they ask me questions about the subject they are studying that I don't know the answer to?* are very common.

The scheme co-ordinator will need to hold regular informal meetings of mentors (two or three a term is sufficient) to allow them to share experiences, ask questions about how other mentors are getting on and share ideas. This doesn't involve disclosing confidences but focuses upon the mentoring process.

Information for the mentors

Mentors need a set of procedural guidelines related to:

- How the school day is made up (length of lessons, breaks, etc)
- Who to contact in the school relating to specific issues
- How meetings are arranged and confirmed
- If someone cannot make a meeting, who informs who
- Health and safety issues relevant to the school and its premises

Additional information can be included according to the nature of the mentoring and those involved.

Additional support

Other forms of support for the mentors:

- Mini-seminars which could include, one or two hours additional training at the request of the mentors
- Newsletters are useful for keeping your mentors informed of meetings, books, videos and events, especially if mentors are from the wider community or from more than one organisation
- *Keep in touch* phone calls to check that all is going well with the mentoring are especially valuable to identify problems at an early stage. (This is best done by the scheme co-ordinator in their capacity as the mentor's *mentor*)

Remember, volunteers do not have to give of their time and, should they feel isolated or not valued, they will vote with their feet and are unlikely to volunteer again!

Good practice guidelines

Schools need to provide mentors with clear guidance regarding current legislation around child protection. Essential elements include:

- The mentor has a legal obligation to report to the school's appointed person (this person should be identified at the training) cases where the youngster relates instances of past and/or current abuse (physical, sexual or psychological)
- All meetings between mentor and mentee must take place during the school day and on the school premises
- Workplace visits can occur but signed parental consent must be gained. The school must satisfy itself that all the travel details and any health and safety issues related to the workplace being visited are resolved
- Meetings must take place in a semi-public environment. If meetings are held in an office or room not also occupied by others, it should not be in an isolated part of the school and the door should remain open for the duration of the meeting. A good rule is, *a private setting within a public space*

Whilst these points may seem strange to those used to an adult workplace, they are as much to protect the mentor as the mentee. All aspects of the mentoring must be transparent and not open to misinterpretation by a third party.

Introduction

 The Mentoring Process

 Peer Mentors

 Volunteer Mentors

 Learning Mentors ◄

 E-Mentoring

 Further Information

Learning Mentors

What is a learning mentor?

There are in the region of 15,000 learning mentors in schools across the UK.
Initially the programme was introduced across six cities: London, Leeds, Birmingham, Manchester, Liverpool and Sheffield.

Currently, learning mentors are appointed by a school to enable its pupils to reach their full potential. They are trained by the LEA and supported by a lead mentor or line manager. The scheme is managed through LEAs and supported through government funding as part of the Excellence in Cities programme. Its main aim is to remove barriers to students' learning and to raise attainment levels. It focuses mainly on young people in key stage 3, although there are local variations.

The initial training normally lasts for a week and involves:

- Mentoring skills and abilities
- Communication skills
- Understanding curriculum issues
- Understanding key issues a pupil may raise

What is a learning mentor?

Learning mentors are essentially educational practitioners. They come from all walks of life and are paid. They work with school staff and pupils, mainly outside the classroom – in the playground, the corridor or in an office.

Often the head of year will give the learning mentor names of pupils whom they feel need support. The learning mentor will assess the students and then work with them to support them in their learning. Sometimes, a young person may refer themselves.

In some cases learning mentors work with those waiting for a place or returning to school after a period of absence. Their aim is to raise standards by removing barriers to learning for individual students and their families. They can act as a bridge between home and school. They work to reduce rates of exclusion and to improve pupils':

- Life chances
- Educational attendance
- Attainment

Differences between learning mentors and volunteer mentors

Learning Mentors

Employed as members of staff

Work one-to-one or in small groups

Focus on removing barriers to educational progress

Deal with issues outside the classroom

Volunteer Mentors

Volunteer from the community or business

Work one-to-one

Focus on a wide range of issues raised by the pupil

Work with the pupil's agenda

Sometimes a learning mentor may work with volunteer mentors. The ground covered by both may be similar.

What do learning mentors deal with?

Schools are under pressure to perform and meet the requirements of targets and league tables. Sometimes, the pupils feel this pressure and it affects their motivation and behaviour.

There are other issues which relate to:

- School work
- Homework clubs
- Behavioural issues
- Lateness and timekeeping
- Relationships and social issues
- Life skills
- Home

The learning mentor is there to explore these with the young person.

What don't learning mentors deal with?

Sometimes schools expect learning mentors to deal with educational and classroom-based issues.

The school may expect the learning mentor to:

- Be an extra pair of hands in the classroom
- Be a security guard
- Be a classroom assistant
- Supervise detention
- Keep discipline at break times
- Be an administrative assistant

These are **NOT** part of the learning mentor's role.

Views from the mentors

'The teachers are under too much pressure
and don't have time to properly deal with some issues.
We deal with stuff outside of the classroom. Sometimes if a youngster
is late one morning, we can deal with that straight away, find out
what it's all about. This can set the youngster up for the
rest of day and make all the difference.'
A learning mentor

'It is important that the
young person feels in control.
Many see the adult as the authority
figure. We break that down through talk
and help them to deal with the anger and
resentment they may feel. We have to
nurture mutual respect and 'go'
with their agenda.'
A learning mentor

'One of my mentees
was on report. We talked about
that and by the end of the week he had
three 'excellents'. He came to me and said,
"Now then mate, we've done it." I said,
"No, **you've** done it. I'm just a part of it."
A learning mentor

Learning mentors: what's the process?

Parents/carers have to agree to their child having a learning mentor.

After the agreement is received, the learning mentor will build trust and rapport and make an agreement with the pupil. Often they will agree the key topic for discussion and the pupil will set themselves some targets within this key topic.

The learning mentor may work one-to-one or in groups depending on the topic and issue.

Skills and benefits

The learning mentor needs to be good at **communicating**. She or he needs to be able to talk to staff, to parents and let them know about the scheme and how they can support it. In the early stages, the learning mentor needs to market him or herself to all interested parties to let them know what is involved and to highlight the potential benefits.

The benefits for pupils of having a learning mentor include:

✔ Improved self-esteem
✔ Improved confidence
✔ Improved social and interpersonal abilities
✔ Improved learning and attainment
✔ Improved behaviour in the classroom and around school
✔ Reduced truancy
✔ Reduced exclusion rates

Views from the mentors

'The young person benefits, the school benefits, the community benefits, future employers benefit (by the youngsters being ready for work) and, of course, the mentors gain a great deal of job satisfaction.'
A learning mentor

'Talk to anyone associated with that young person; they will notice the difference.'
A learning mentor

'They need someone to say, "Yeah, you're doing it right"; you know, give them approval for doing it right.'
Learning mentor

'We have to meet the youngster on their terms, on their ground and accept their differences.'
Learning mentor

Introduction

 The
Mentoring
Process

 Peer
Mentors

 Volunteer
Mentors

 Learning
Mentors

 E-Mentoring ◀

 Further
Information

E-Mentoring

Overview of e-mentoring

With the advent of new technologies, e-mentoring is one of the newest developments in the mentoring process. E-mentoring can have huge advantages where the mentoring pair may not be able to meet face-to-face regularly.

E-mail is an appropriate technology for the age group, given possible low boredom thresholds and low personal motivation in the mentee.

E-mentoring can enhance time management and general IT skills.

Because of its *distance*, e-mentoring has the potential to give support without embarrassment or inhibition.

Good practice guidelines

Applying some ground rules will enhance the likelihood of the
e-relationship being successful.

- Both parties should meet at least once (three face-to face-meetings is ideal) before the e-mentoring begins
- The scheme co-ordinator needs to brief both parties about the boundaries of the relationship and establish ground rules of appropriate behaviour
- Where the mentee is vulnerable or at risk, the scheme co-ordinator will need to be included in all correspondence (this is likely to be rare as face-to-face mentoring will be more successful with this target group). The scheme co-ordinator has ultimate responsibility and being included in the correspondence is a protection for those concerned

Good practice guidelines

- If one of the parties is dyslexic or has other learning difficulties it is important that the scheme co-ordinator provides support and information, so that writing an e-mail doesn't become humiliating or embarrassing. (If they are both dyslexic then it can be quite liberating for the mentee)
- The mentee and mentor will need regular access to appropriate technologies
- The mentor and mentee should agree the timescales for checking and exchanging e-mails. (Once a week? Daily? Fortnightly?)
- There is scope for misunderstanding written e-mails so create an e-mail etiquette checklist
- The mentor needs to understand the value of reflecting and summarising online. This helps to avoid making assumptions that the mentee has understood something when they haven't, or the mentee agreeing just so as not to offend or appear stupid

Further Information

Standards

Mentoring is still evolving as a professional activity but standards are now available and generally take two forms:

- Benchmarking of existing practice for mentors
- Scheme co-ordinators' standards

The European Mentoring and Coaching Council has a comprehensive list of standards. These can be adapted for a variety of contexts.

Mentors' standards
The number of programmes for mentors is growing: those on the following pages range from the new National Vocational Qualification (NVQ) for Mentoring, to a Masters degree.

Standards

Certificate in Mentoring and Coaching – Four NVQ units at level 4
This is part of the Training & Development NVQ by the Chartered Institute of Personnel and Development (CIPD) and is part of their suite of vocational qualifications. Successful candidates can also gain the remaining units for the full qualification – this can include the NVQ assessor units. Further details can be obtained from the CIPD or the Greenwood Partnership (contact details on page 110).

Mentoring in the Community – Certificate and Diploma programmes
These accredited courses are run by the Mentoring and Active Citizenship Unit at Middlesex University and are for existing scheme co-ordinators and those moving from individual mentoring to scheme management. Tel: 020 8362 6846
E-mail: j.iremonger@mdx.ac.uk

MSc in Mentoring and Coaching
This part-time or full-time Masters degree is designed for those working with change whether as a mentor, scheme co-ordinator or at a more strategic level, or initiating change in communities or organisations. Contact: Sheffield Hallam University, Postgraduate Programmes Office. Tel: 0114 225 2820
E-mail: sbf@shu.ac.uk   www.shu.ac.uk/schools/sbf

Standards (cont'd)

Scheme standards

Approved Provider Standard
A benchmarking process for organisations involved in initiating and running volunteer mentoring schemes, funded by the Active Community Unit of the Home Office and the DfES. Mentoring programmes dependent on government funding will at some point in the future be required to demonstrate commitment to these standards as a condition of funding (no date has yet been indicated when this is likely to be introduced). This Standard is being promoted and administered by The Mentoring and Befriending Foundation on behalf of the government. Contact: The Mentoring and Befriending Foundation on page 110.

Excellence in Mentoring for Schools
Similar to the Approved Provider Standard but adjusted to meet the needs of schools and those in schools who rely on a third party to recruit and train mentors. This is most applicable to schools that work closely with their local Education Business Partnership or have an on-going relationship with a local organisation that recruits and trains their own employees to mentor. Contact: The Mentoring and Befriending Foundation on page 110.

Books

***On Track* by The Greenwood Partnership**
Designed to take you through every stage of designing your own peer mentoring scheme, this pack contains: a scheme co-ordinator's manual, trainer's pack and CD-Rom to support young mentors.

***The Mentoring Pocketbook* by Geof Alred, Bob Garvey and Richard Smith**
Published by Management Pocketbooks Ltd, UK
For mentors and mentees, a pocketful of tips and techniques to maximise the benefits of this highly effective development process.

***Mentoring Students and Young People* by Andrew Miller**
Published by Kogan Page, UK
This book presents a range of case studies and key findings in setting up and running mentoring schemes in education in the UK and North America.

Videos and DVDs

Peer Mentoring – **The Greenwood Partnership**
This DVD-ROM contains everything you need to start, set up and run your own school peer mentoring scheme. It includes:
- Peer Mentoring – a film illustrating the benefits of peer mentoring
- An interactive guide to peer mentoring
- Scheme Co-ordinator's Pack and Trainer's Pack (PDF files)

Learning mentors – **The Greenwood Partnership**
This two-video boxed set introduces the role and skills of learning mentors and then illustrates how they differ from teachers and classroom assistants.

New Chances, New Horizons – **The Greenwood Partnership**
A two-video boxed set that looks at how mentoring has enabled 18 to 20-year-olds re-engage in the learning process and develop options in their lives.

Face to face – **National Mentoring Network**
Introduces the benefits of mentoring in schools, including details of organisations with volunteers in schools.

Websites

www.nebpn.org
The National Education Business Partnership (EBP) Network is the umbrella organisation and national voice for 138 EBPs working in 11 regions.

www.mandbf.org.uk
The Mentoring and Befriending Foundation.
A good source of information and support.

www.ebp.org.uk
EBP regions in Scotland.

www.standards.dfes.gov.uk/excellence/
This DfES website contains information on the Excellence in Cities initiative and on learning mentors.

www.homeoffice.gov.uk/acu/acu.htm
Site for the Active Community Unit (ACU) of the Home Office and contains information relevant to community groups using mentoring.

www.simonmidgley.co.uk/mentoring
This is a site with information and links on mentoring is schools and the community.

Contact addresses

The Greenwood Partnership is involved in all facets of mentoring including designing schemes, training mentors, research, evaluation and the design of paper-based, video and CD-Rom learning materials.

The Greenwood Partnership
67 Prospect Road, St Albans AL1 2AU
Tel: 07957 380157
E-mail: info@greenwood-partnership.com Web: www.greenwood-partnership.com

The Mentoring and Befriending Foundation exists to promote mentoring in education and the community. There is a regional network, newsletter and the Foundation publishes a range of information handouts and evaluation reports.

Web: www.mandbf.org.uk

Let's Twist/Jive Partners – 6th form, young women and undergraduates into engineering and science careers.

Web: http://letstwist.bradfordcollege.ac.uk/

About the authors

Bob Garvey

Bob has been involved in education all his career. His experience includes primary and secondary education as a teacher and he now works in higher education as a principal lecturer at Sheffield Hallam University. In 1998 Bob was awarded a PhD from The University of Durham for his research into mentoring. He has published widely on the topic of mentoring in academic and professional journals and has contributed chapters to a number of edited books. Bob is co-author of the best-selling *Mentoring Pocketbook*.

Kim Langridge

Kim has been involved in mentoring for many years both as a mentor and a mentee. He has written many scheme co-ordinators' handbooks for a range of organisations including schools, voluntary sector groups and business organisations. He provides training for mentors, mentees and scheme co-ordinators throughout the UK. He is currently involved in a mentoring project targeting young offenders. Kim is interested in all aspects of human learning and development. He holds a Masters degree in Strategic Human Resources Development from London Guildhall University.

Order Form

Your details

Name _____

Position _____

School _____

Address _____

_____

_____

Telephone _____

Fax _____

E-mail _____

VAT No. (EC only) _____

Your Order Ref _____

Please send me:

		No. copies
Pupil Mentoring	Pocketbook	☐
_____	Pocketbook	☐
_____	Pocketbook	☐
_____	Pocketbook	☐
_____	Pocketbook	☐

Order by Post

Teachers' Pocketbooks

Laurel House, Station Approach
Alresford, Hants. SO24 9JH UK

Order by Phone, Fax or Internet

Telephone: +44 (0)1962 735573
Facsimile: +44 (0)1962 733637
E-mail: sales@teacherspocketbooks.co.uk
Web: www.teacherspocketbooks.co.uk